W9-AHB-379

Poetry Builders

Rena and Rio Build a
RHYME

by Pamela Hall
illustrated by Cary Pillo

Content Consultant
Kris Bigalk
Director of Creative Writing
Normandale Community College

NORWOOD HOUSE PRESS
CHICAGO, ILLINOIS

Norwood House Press
P.O. Box 316598
Chicago, Illinois 60631
For information regarding Norwood House Press, please visit
our website at:
www.norwoodhousepress.com or call 866-565-2900.

Editor: Melissa York
Designer: Emily Love
Project Management: Red Line Editorial

Library of Congress Cataloging-in-Publication Data
Hall, Pamela, 1961-
  Rena and Rio build a rhyme / by Pamela Hall ; illustrated by
Cary Pillo.
      p. cm. -- (Poetry builders)
  Includes bibliographical references.
  Summary: "Two friends visit a candy shop and have treats
while learning how to write poems that rhyme. Includes
creative writing exercises to assist the reader in writing poems
that rhyme"--Provided by publisher.
  ISBN-13: 978-1-59953-439-8 (library ed. : alk. paper)
  ISBN-10: 1-59953-439-8 (library ed. : alk. paper)
  1. Rhyme--Juvenile literature. 2. Rhyme--Juvenile fiction. I.
Pillo, Cary, ill. II. Title.
  PN1059.R5H35 2011
  808.1--dc22
                                    2010043869

Manufactured in the United States of America in
North Mankato, Minnesota.
286R—082015

Words in **black bold** are defined in the glossary.

"Why I Love Writing Poems"

I love to write about my life. I always have so much to say! Dad thinks this is a great way to get all my insides out. He says don't worry if the words tumble so fast they don't make sense at first. There's time to fix them later. That's called **revising**.

I write different kinds of poems. Most of them rhyme. I collect words that go together so that my poems flow like music.

Dad says I have a "unique voice." I think that's because nobody else sounds just like me. Maybe someday I'll put my poems into a book for kids to read. Then I'll be able to tell the world how Black Jack Cherry ice cream tastes or how it felt when I got my kitten, Squeaky.

By Rena, age 10

"Hey, Rio, it's Rena at the door," called Rio's mom.

"Yeah, we're going to the candy store!" replied Rio, zipping outside to his friend.

"That was a great rhyme!" Rena exclaimed.

"What was?" Rio asked.

"When your mom said,
Hey Rio, it's Rena at the door,
you said, *Yeah, we're going to the candy store!*
Door rhymes with store. You've written the beginning
of a rhyme poem!" Rena said, as she took off on her
bike.

"Cool!" Rio pedaled after her. "And I've got two more lines:

Now I'm riding on my bike

To go get candy that I like!"

"Hey, I like it!" exclaimed Rena.

"Did you know you can make your poem rhyme with different patterns?" Rena added. "Your rhyme was AABB. That means the first two lines rhyme, and then the next two lines rhyme. Door and store. Bike and like. See?"

"Oh, like Twinkle, Twinkle . . . " Rio started singing:

"Twinkle, twinkle, little star,

How I wonder what you are

Up above the world so high

Like a diamond in the sky."

"That's it!" exclaimed Rena. "Star and are, and high and sky."

The two screeched to a stop outside the candy store. Rio locked their bikes to a bike rack as Rena pulled out her notebook.

"See this, Rio?" Rena pointed at her notebook. "My new poem is ABAB. See? The rhymes skip a line."

Cats are sneaky
And cats are sly.
But I love Squeaky.
I don't know why.

Rio laughed. "I can imagine Squeaky sneaking down your stairs!"

The two pushed open the door to the candy shop and walked in.

The store owner, Manny, waved a huge chocolate bunny from behind the counter. "Hi, Rena and Rio! It's great to see you today!"

"Wow." Rena breathed in the sweet smells.

Raspberry sours glistened in glass jars. Licorice ropes tangled around tubs of gummy bears. Swirled lollypops marched in rows near blocks of chocolate.

The two wandered around trying to decide what to buy. Rena finally picked licorice whips, tangy taffy, and a candy necklace. Rio grabbed bubble gum, a block of fudge, and a sucker shaped like a rocket.

Rio and Rena stepped up to the counter to pay.

Rio chanted,

"Taffy, fudge, and lollypop,

Wish I didn't have to stop!"

"I like your **end rhyme**," said Manny, putting Rio's candy in a bag.

"End rhyme?" asked Rio.

"Here," Manny said, handing Rio a napkin and a pen. "Write down your poem."

"Okay." Rio shrugged a little, but he did it anyway. He held out his poem.

Taffy, fudge, and lollypop,
Wish I didn't have to stop!

"See where your rhyme is?" Manny said. "Lollypop and stop are at the *ends* of the lines. It's an end rhyme."

"You can make ABAB or AABB patterns with different end rhymes," added Rena.

"I get it," Rio said. "Thanks, Manny!"

Rio leaned against the counter. "Do all poems rhyme at the end?" he asked, pulling his fudge out of the bag.

"No, just my favorites. I can make a rhyme without even tryin'." Rena giggled a little at her own joke. "But even I like to play with the rules. See?"

Rena opened her journal and flipped to a page that said "Christmas." She passed it to Rio so he could read her poem.

Our tree shines bright with sparkly light,
I hope Santa brings me a bike.

"Light and bike don't rhyme perfectly, but they sound good together," Rio noticed.

"Good job, Rio!" Manny said. "That's called a **near rhyme**."

"And bright and light in the first line rhyme, too," pointed out Rio. "Did you do that on purpose, Rena?"

"Sure did!" Rena said.

"That's called an **inner rhyme**," Manny added.

"Like, My dog caught a frog on a jog. See how the rhyme hides inside the line?" Rena explained.

"Or: I smudged your page with fudge," Rio grinned, licking his fingers. "That's a near rhyme, too."

19

Rena and Rio left the store and headed to the park.

Rena started flipping through her journal. "Want to see some of my favorite rhyming creations?"

"Sure," Rio said.

The two friends bent over the notebook.

Scrubbing, bubbly in the tub,
I washed off grease and grime and grub.

Rotten socks and bent-up pens
My messy floor just never ends.

Alarm clock jingle jangles
My jammies caught in tangles.
I think I have to tinkle,
My face has sleepy wrinkles!

A spelling list, a single sock
Some moldy cheese, an awesome rock
A clump of grass, a rubber cricket
A bag of acorns, an old lunch ticket
Last Wednesday's homework, a banana peel—
It's amazing what my backpack will reveal!

"Let's write some more rhymes! I brought my Rhyming Dictionary," said Rena, digging in her backpack. "It takes the ends of words and matches them with all the words they'll rhyme with."

She found the book and waved it in the air. "Pick a word, any word."

"Gum!" Rio said, chewing away.

"Ha, that's easy," Rena said. "I just look up UM. *Bum, chum, crumb, drum, dumb*— there are lots of rhymes. It even lists longer words like *cranium* and *aluminum*."

"*Your cranium*

is filled with bubble gum!" Rio chanted.

"Uh, good job, I think," Rena said, wrinkling her nose. "Let's write that one down."

"What else?" Rio said. "I don't have another idea for a poem."

"Let's write down what we see," said Rena. "I like to start my rhymes with a list and then rearrange things until it's a poem."

"OK," said Rio. "I'll write down our ideas."

Babies lick ice cream cones
Their mothers wipe their faces
People talking on cell phones hurrying
        down the street
Cars honking their horns
Sunshine
Chirping birds

When they were done, they stared at their list for a while.

"Hmm, let me think," said Rena. "Cones rhymes with phones, so I want to use that somehow . . ."

"I like the part about baby's faces," Rio said. "But what rhymes with faces?"

Rio started making a list: *aces, laces, traces, places.*

"Aha!" Rio said, and he started writing even faster. As Rena looked over his shoulder, he wrote and erased and wrote and erased.

Rio jumped up at last. "It's done!" he exclaimed. He showed Rena the page.

Babies lick at ice cream cones,
Their mothers wipe their faces.
People chat and text on phones,
Going busy places.

"Bravo!" Rena clapped. "An ABAB rhyme. Maybe I'll get you a journal for your birthday," she teased. "I'll autograph it first because I'm a famous writer."

"So am I," Rio laughed, signing his name on Rena's journal. "Here's my next rhyme:

Race you back to Maple Street

I'm the one you need to beat!"

You Can Write a Rhyme, too!

Some poems have end rhyme. End rhymes come in different patterns. In AABB poems, the first two lines and the last two lines rhyme. In ABAB patterns, the rhymes skip a line.

You can write a rhyme about anything you like. To get started, try free writing. Just write as fast as you can about something. Try free writing about your favorite food—maybe pickles.

Pickles, green with little bumps like warts, more brownish-green, maybe, and sour and dripping wet. Sometimes spicy. Pickle feeling stays on my tongue. Grandpa grows cucumbers for pickles in his garden. Have to pick them before they're too big!

Revise your favorite parts.

Pickles are sour on my tongue.

What words rhyme with tongue? (If you need help, check a rhyming dictionary.)

sung, young, sprung, clung, among, lung

Can you think of another line to rhyme with tongue?
Maybe:

Grandma picks cukes when they're young.

Hmm. Maybe that's not quite right. You might have to change your first line to find a better rhyme:

Pickles bumpy, pickles green
I devour them like a machine!

Or, maybe:

Pickles, bumpy, green, and wet
I can eat a dozen—no sweat!

Remember, the writing is the most important part. Don't worry about getting it exactly right the first time. Keep at it! The perfect word will come to you.

Glossary

end rhyme: rhyme at the ends of lines in a poem.

inner rhyme: rhyme hidden inside a line of poetry.

near rhyme: words in a poem that sound alike but don't rhyme perfectly.

revising: changing and rewriting a written work until you are satisfied with it.

For More Information

Books

Lanksy, Bruce. *My Teacher's in Detention: Kids' Favorite Funny School Poems*. Minnetonka, MN: Meadowbrook Press, 2006.

Prelutsky, Jack. *Be Glad Your Nose Is on Your Face and Other Poems: Some of the Best of Jack Prelutsky*. New York: Greenwillow Books, 2008.

Websites

The Children's Poetry Archive
www.poetryarchive.org/childrensarchive/home.do
This website includes many fun rhyming poems.

Giggle Poetry
www.gigglepoetry.com/
This website has lots of information about rhyming poems.

Rhyme Zone
www.rhymezone.com
This website is a rhyming dictionary. Enter any word and it will produce many words that rhyme with it.

About the Author

Pamela Hall lives in Lakeland, Minnesota with her children and her dog. She has published 15 books so far.

About the Illustrator

Cary Pillo lives in Seattle, Washington. Her number-one all-time favorite candy is fancy chocolate.